DECEMBER CALENDAR

Sunday	Monday	Tuesday	Wednesday	Thursday	Friday	Saturday

CHRISTMAS CALENDAR

December 23

December 24 - CHRISTMAS EVE

December 25 - CHRISTMAS DAY

December 26 - BOXING DAY

December 27

December 28

If lost, please return to:

_____

It's beginning to look
a lot like Christmas....

GOALS & SPECIAL PLANS FOR THE CHRISTMAS SEASON

GOALS & SPECIAL PLANS FOR THE CHRISTMAS SEASON

NOVEMBER CALENDAR

Sunday	Monday	Tuesday	Wednesday	Thursday	Friday	Saturday

NEW YEAR'S CALENDAR

December 29

December 30

December 31 – NEW YEAR'S EVE

January 1 – NEW YEAR'S DAY

January 2

CHRISTMAS TO DO LIST

- [ ]
- [ ]
- [ ]
- [ ]
- [ ]
- [ ]
- [ ]
- [ ]
- [ ]
- [ ]
- [ ]
- [ ]
- [ ]
- [ ]
- [ ]
- [ ]
- [ ]
- [ ]
- [ ]
- [ ]
- [ ]
- [ ]
- [ ]
- [ ]
- [ ]
- [ ]

CHRISTMAS TO DO LIST

- [ ]
- [ ]
- [ ]
- [ ]
- [ ]
- [ ]
- [ ]
- [ ]
- [ ]
- [ ]
- [ ]
- [ ]
- [ ]
- [ ]
- [ ]
- [ ]
- [ ]
- [ ]
- [ ]
- [ ]
- [ ]
- [ ]
- [ ]
- [ ]
- [ ]
- [ ]
- [ ]
- [ ]

CHRISTMAS TO DO LIST

- [ ]
- [ ]
- [ ]
- [ ]
- [ ]
- [ ]
- [ ]
- [ ]
- [ ]
- [ ]
- [ ]
- [ ]
- [ ]
- [ ]
- [ ]
- [ ]
- [ ]
- [ ]
- [ ]
- [ ]
- [ ]
- [ ]
- [ ]
- [ ]
- [ ]
- [ ]

CHRISTMAS TRADITIONS / BUCKET LIST

☐ _____

☐ _____

☐ _____

☐ _____

☐ _____

☐ _____

☐ _____

☐ _____

☐ _____

☐ _____

☐ _____

☐ _____

☐ _____

☐ _____

☐ _____

☐ _____

☐ _____

☐ _____

☐ _____

☐ _____

☐ _____

☐ _____

☐ _____

☐ _____

☐ _____

Suggestions
Go Sledding
Decorate Cookies
Decorate a Christmas Tree
See Christmas Lights
Make Hot Chocolate
Go Christmas Carolling
Read the Christmas Story
Serve at a Soup Kitchen
Donate Gifts to Charity
Go Ice Skating
Write a Letter to Santa
Make Paper Snowflakes
Christmas Movie Marathon
Build a Snowman
Make a Gingerbread House
Make Snow Angels
Go to Church
Take Pictures by the Tree
Ugly Sweaters
Write a Christmas Letter
Go to a Christmas Concert
Elf on the Shelf
Advent Calendar
Cookie Exchange Party
New Year's Resolutions

CHRISTMAS PHOTO PLANNER

Item	Notes		
PLAN PHOTOS			
Schedule Photographer			
Date			
Location			
Plan Outfits			
Plan Poses			
Order Prints?			
Email Delivery?			
Get Cards Made Up?			
Photo Sizes			
Number of Photos			
Notes			

CHRISTMAS LETTER PLANNER

PLAN LETTER	
Item	Notes
Date	
Decoration?	
Ideas to Include	

Notes for each Family Member	
Name	Ideas

CHRISTMAS CARD TRACKER

CARD ADDRESS DETAILS	YEAR			
Name Address Email	Sent ☐	Sent ☐	Sent ☐	Sent ☐
	Rec'd ☐	Rec'd ☐	Rec'd ☐	Rec'd ☐
Name Address Email	Sent ☐	Sent ☐	Sent ☐	Sent ☐
	Rec'd ☐	Rec'd ☐	Rec'd ☐	Rec'd ☐
Name Address Email	Sent ☐	Sent ☐	Sent ☐	Sent ☐
	Rec'd ☐	Rec'd ☐	Rec'd ☐	Rec'd ☐
Name Address Email	Sent ☐	Sent ☐	Sent ☐	Sent ☐
	Rec'd ☐	Rec'd ☐	Rec'd ☐	Rec'd ☐
Name Address Email	Sent ☐	Sent ☐	Sent ☐	Sent ☐
	Rec'd ☐	Rec'd ☐	Rec'd ☐	Rec'd ☐
Name Address Email	Sent ☐	Sent ☐	Sent ☐	Sent ☐
	Rec'd ☐	Rec'd ☐	Rec'd ☐	Rec'd ☐

CHRISTMAS CARD TRACKER

CARD ADDRESS DETAILS	YEAR			
Name Address Email	Sent ☐	Sent ☐	Sent ☐	Sent ☐
	Rec'd ☐	Rec'd ☐	Rec'd ☐	Rec'd ☐
Name Address Email	Sent ☐	Sent ☐	Sent ☐	Sent ☐
	Rec'd ☐	Rec'd ☐	Rec'd ☐	Rec'd ☐
Name Address Email	Sent ☐	Sent ☐	Sent ☐	Sent ☐
	Rec'd ☐	Rec'd ☐	Rec'd ☐	Rec'd ☐
Name Address Email	Sent ☐	Sent ☐	Sent ☐	Sent ☐
	Rec'd ☐	Rec'd ☐	Rec'd ☐	Rec'd ☐
Name Address Email	Sent ☐	Sent ☐	Sent ☐	Sent ☐
	Rec'd ☐	Rec'd ☐	Rec'd ☐	Rec'd ☐
Name Address Email	Sent ☐	Sent ☐	Sent ☐	Sent ☐
	Rec'd ☐	Rec'd ☐	Rec'd ☐	Rec'd ☐

CHRISTMAS CARD TRACKER

CARD ADDRESS DETAILS	YEAR			
Name	Sent ☐	Sent ☐	Sent ☐	Sent ☐
Address				
	Rec'd ☐	Rec'd ☐	Rec'd ☐	Rec'd ☐
Email				
Name	Sent ☐	Sent ☐	Sent ☐	Sent ☐
Address				
	Rec'd ☐	Rec'd ☐	Rec'd ☐	Rec'd ☐
Email				
Name	Sent ☐	Sent ☐	Sent ☐	Sent ☐
Address				
	Rec'd ☐	Rec'd ☐	Rec'd ☐	Rec'd ☐
Email				
Name	Sent ☐	Sent ☐	Sent ☐	Sent ☐
Address				
	Rec'd ☐	Rec'd ☐	Rec'd ☐	Rec'd ☐
Email				
Name	Sent ☐	Sent ☐	Sent ☐	Sent ☐
Address				
	Rec'd ☐	Rec'd ☐	Rec'd ☐	Rec'd ☐
Email				
Name	Sent ☐	Sent ☐	Sent ☐	Sent ☐
Address				
	Rec'd ☐	Rec'd ☐	Rec'd ☐	Rec'd ☐
Email				

CHRISTMAS CARD TRACKER

CARD ADDRESS DETAILS	YEAR			
Name Address Email	Sent ☐	Sent ☐	Sent ☐	Sent ☐
	Rec'd ☐	Rec'd ☐	Rec'd ☐	Rec'd ☐
Name Address Email	Sent ☐	Sent ☐	Sent ☐	Sent ☐
	Rec'd ☐	Rec'd ☐	Rec'd ☐	Rec'd ☐
Name Address Email	Sent ☐	Sent ☐	Sent ☐	Sent ☐
	Rec'd ☐	Rec'd ☐	Rec'd ☐	Rec'd ☐
Name Address Email	Sent ☐	Sent ☐	Sent ☐	Sent ☐
	Rec'd ☐	Rec'd ☐	Rec'd ☐	Rec'd ☐
Name Address Email	Sent ☐	Sent ☐	Sent ☐	Sent ☐
	Rec'd ☐	Rec'd ☐	Rec'd ☐	Rec'd ☐
Name Address Email	Sent ☐	Sent ☐	Sent ☐	Sent ☐
	Rec'd ☐	Rec'd ☐	Rec'd ☐	Rec'd ☐

CHRISTMAS CARD TRACKER

CARD ADDRESS DETAILS	YEAR			
Name	Sent ☐	Sent ☐	Sent ☐	Sent ☐
Address				
	Rec'd ☐	Rec'd ☐	Rec'd ☐	Rec'd ☐
Email				
Name	Sent ☐	Sent ☐	Sent ☐	Sent ☐
Address				
	Rec'd ☐	Rec'd ☐	Rec'd ☐	Rec'd ☐
Email				
Name	Sent ☐	Sent ☐	Sent ☐	Sent ☐
Address				
	Rec'd ☐	Rec'd ☐	Rec'd ☐	Rec'd ☐
Email				
Name	Sent ☐	Sent ☐	Sent ☐	Sent ☐
Address				
	Rec'd ☐	Rec'd ☐	Rec'd ☐	Rec'd ☐
Email				
Name	Sent ☐	Sent ☐	Sent ☐	Sent ☐
Address				
	Rec'd ☐	Rec'd ☐	Rec'd ☐	Rec'd ☐
Email				
Name	Sent ☐	Sent ☐	Sent ☐	Sent ☐
Address				
	Rec'd ☐	Rec'd ☐	Rec'd ☐	Rec'd ☐
Email				

CHRISTMAS CARD TRACKER

CARD ADDRESS DETAILS	YEAR			
Name Address Email	Sent ☐	Sent ☐	Sent ☐	Sent ☐
	Rec'd ☐	Rec'd ☐	Rec'd ☐	Rec'd ☐
Name Address Email	Sent ☐	Sent ☐	Sent ☐	Sent ☐
	Rec'd ☐	Rec'd ☐	Rec'd ☐	Rec'd ☐
Name Address Email	Sent ☐	Sent ☐	Sent ☐	Sent ☐
	Rec'd ☐	Rec'd ☐	Rec'd ☐	Rec'd ☐
Name Address Email	Sent ☐	Sent ☐	Sent ☐	Sent ☐
	Rec'd ☐	Rec'd ☐	Rec'd ☐	Rec'd ☐
Name Address Email	Sent ☐	Sent ☐	Sent ☐	Sent ☐
	Rec'd ☐	Rec'd ☐	Rec'd ☐	Rec'd ☐
Name Address Email	Sent ☐	Sent ☐	Sent ☐	Sent ☐
	Rec'd ☐	Rec'd ☐	Rec'd ☐	Rec'd ☐

CHRISTMAS CARD TRACKER

CARD ADDRESS DETAILS	YEAR			
Name	Sent ☐	Sent ☐	Sent ☐	Sent ☐
Address				
	Rec'd ☐	Rec'd ☐	Rec'd ☐	Rec'd ☐
Email				
Name	Sent ☐	Sent ☐	Sent ☐	Sent ☐
Address				
	Rec'd ☐	Rec'd ☐	Rec'd ☐	Rec'd ☐
Email				
Name	Sent ☐	Sent ☐	Sent ☐	Sent ☐
Address				
	Rec'd ☐	Rec'd ☐	Rec'd ☐	Rec'd ☐
Email				
Name	Sent ☐	Sent ☐	Sent ☐	Sent ☐
Address				
	Rec'd ☐	Rec'd ☐	Rec'd ☐	Rec'd ☐
Email				
Name	Sent ☐	Sent ☐	Sent ☐	Sent ☐
Address				
	Rec'd ☐	Rec'd ☐	Rec'd ☐	Rec'd ☐
Email				
Name	Sent ☐	Sent ☐	Sent ☐	Sent ☐
Address				
	Rec'd ☐	Rec'd ☐	Rec'd ☐	Rec'd ☐
Email				

CHRISTMAS CARD TRACKER

CARD ADDRESS DETAILS	YEAR			
Name	Sent ☐	Sent ☐	Sent ☐	Sent ☐
Address				
	Rec'd ☐	Rec'd ☐	Rec'd ☐	Rec'd ☐
Email				
Name	Sent ☐	Sent ☐	Sent ☐	Sent ☐
Address				
	Rec'd ☐	Rec'd ☐	Rec'd ☐	Rec'd ☐
Email				
Name	Sent ☐	Sent ☐	Sent ☐	Sent ☐
Address				
	Rec'd ☐	Rec'd ☐	Rec'd ☐	Rec'd ☐
Email				
Name	Sent ☐	Sent ☐	Sent ☐	Sent ☐
Address				
	Rec'd ☐	Rec'd ☐	Rec'd ☐	Rec'd ☐
Email				
Name	Sent ☐	Sent ☐	Sent ☐	Sent ☐
Address				
	Rec'd ☐	Rec'd ☐	Rec'd ☐	Rec'd ☐
Email				
Name	Sent ☐	Sent ☐	Sent ☐	Sent ☐
Address				
	Rec'd ☐	Rec'd ☐	Rec'd ☐	Rec'd ☐
Email				

CHRISTMAS CARD TRACKER

CARD ADDRESS DETAILS	YEAR			
Name Address Email	Sent ☐	Sent ☐	Sent ☐	Sent ☐
	Rec'd ☐	Rec'd ☐	Rec'd ☐	Rec'd ☐
Name Address Email	Sent ☐	Sent ☐	Sent ☐	Sent ☐
	Rec'd ☐	Rec'd ☐	Rec'd ☐	Rec'd ☐
Name Address Email	Sent ☐	Sent ☐	Sent ☐	Sent ☐
	Rec'd ☐	Rec'd ☐	Rec'd ☐	Rec'd ☐
Name Address Email	Sent ☐	Sent ☐	Sent ☐	Sent ☐
	Rec'd ☐	Rec'd ☐	Rec'd ☐	Rec'd ☐
Name Address Email	Sent ☐	Sent ☐	Sent ☐	Sent ☐
	Rec'd ☐	Rec'd ☐	Rec'd ☐	Rec'd ☐
Name Address Email	Sent ☐	Sent ☐	Sent ☐	Sent ☐
	Rec'd ☐	Rec'd ☐	Rec'd ☐	Rec'd ☐

DO IT YOURSELF GIFTS & DÉCOR

PROJECT 1	
Description	
Item is for	
Hours to make	
Tutorial/pattern	
Start by	
Supplies to buy	
Supplies I have	

PROJECT 2	
Description	
Item is for	
Hours to make	
Tutorial/pattern	
Start by	
Supplies to buy	
Supplies I have	

DO IT YOURSELF GIFTS & DÉCOR

PROJECT 3	
Description	
Item is for	
Hours to make	
Tutorial/pattern	
Start by	
Supplies to buy	
Supplies I have	

PROJECT 4	
Description	
Item is for	
Hours to make	
Tutorial/pattern	
Start by	
Supplies to buy	
Supplies I have	

DO IT YOURSELF GIFTS & DÉCOR

PROJECT 5	
Description	
Item is for	
Hours to make	
Tutorial/pattern	
Start by	
Supplies to buy	
Supplies I have	

PROJECT 6	
Description	
Item is for	
Hours to make	
Tutorial/pattern	
Start by	
Supplies to buy	
Supplies I have	

DO IT YOURSELF GIFTS & DÉCOR

PROJECT 7	
Description	
Item is for	
Hours to make	
Tutorial/pattern	
Start by	
Supplies to buy	
Supplies I have	

PROJECT 8	
Description	
Item is for	
Hours to make	
Tutorial/pattern	
Start by	
Supplies to buy	
Supplies I have	

DO IT YOURSELF GIFTS & DÉCOR

PROJECT 9	
Description	
Item is for	
Hours to make	
Tutorial/pattern	
Start by	
Supplies to buy	
Supplies I have	

PROJECT 10	
Description	
Item is for	
Hours to make	
Tutorial/pattern	
Start by	
Supplies to buy	
Supplies I have	

GIFT PLANNER

FAMILY					
Name	Ideas	Sizes	Budget	Purchased	Wrapped
				☐	☐
				☐	☐
				☐	☐
				☐	☐
				☐	☐
				☐	☐
				☐	☐
				☐	☐
				☐	☐
				☐	☐
				☐	☐
				☐	☐
				☐	☐

GIFT PLANNER

FAMILY					
Name	Ideas	Sizes	Budget	Purchased	Wrapped
				☐	☐
				☐	☐
				☐	☐
				☐	☐
				☐	☐
				☐	☐
				☐	☐
				☐	☐
				☐	☐
				☐	☐
				☐	☐
				☐	☐

GIFT PLANNER

FRIENDS					
Name	Ideas	Sizes	Budget	Purchased	Wrapped
				☐	☐
				☐	☐
				☐	☐
				☐	☐
				☐	☐
				☐	☐
				☐	☐
				☐	☐
				☐	☐
				☐	☐
				☐	☐
				☐	☐
				☐	☐

GIFT PLANNER

FRIENDS					
Name	Ideas	Sizes	Budget	Purchased	Wrapped
				☐	☐
				☐	☐
				☐	☐
				☐	☐
				☐	☐
				☐	☐
				☐	☐
				☐	☐
				☐	☐
				☐	☐
				☐	☐
				☐	☐
				☐	☐

GIFT PLANNER

COWORKERS					
Name	Ideas	Sizes	Budget	Purchased	Wrapped
				☐	☐
				☐	☐
				☐	☐
				☐	☐
				☐	☐
				☐	☐
				☐	☐
				☐	☐
				☐	☐
				☐	☐
				☐	☐
				☐	☐
				☐	☐

GIFT PLANNER

NEIGHBORS					
Name	Ideas	Sizes	Budget	Purchased	Wrapped
				☐	☐
				☐	☐
				☐	☐
				☐	☐
				☐	☐
				☐	☐
				☐	☐
				☐	☐
				☐	☐
				☐	☐
				☐	☐
				☐	☐
				☐	☐

GIFT PLANNER

TEACHERS & SCHOOL STAFF					
Name	Ideas	Sizes	Budget	Purchased	Wrapped
				☐	☐
				☐	☐
				☐	☐
				☐	☐
				☐	☐
				☐	☐
				☐	☐
				☐	☐
				☐	☐
				☐	☐
				☐	☐
				☐	☐
				☐	☐

GIFT PLANNER

OTHER PEOPLE & PETS					
Name	Ideas	Sizes	Budget	Purchased	Wrapped
				☐	☐
				☐	☐
				☐	☐
				☐	☐
				☐	☐
				☐	☐
				☐	☐
				☐	☐
				☐	☐
				☐	☐
				☐	☐
				☐	☐
				☐	☐

BLACK FRIDAY SHOPPING LIST

STORE & ADDRESS:

Item	Price	Notes

STORE & ADDRESS:

Item	Price	Notes

STORE & ADDRESS:

Item	Price	Notes

BLACK FRIDAY SHOPPING LIST

STORE & ADDRESS:		
Item	Price	Notes

STORE & ADDRESS:		
Item	Price	Notes

STORE & ADDRESS:		
Item	Price	Notes

CYBER MONDAY SHOPPING LIST

STORE & WEBSITE:		
Item	Price	Notes

STORE & WEBSITE:		
Item	Price	Notes

STORE & WEBSITE:		
Item	Price	Notes

CYBER MONDAY SHOPPING LIST

STORE & WEBSITE:

Item	Price	Notes

STORE & WEBSITE:

Item	Price	Notes

STORE & WEBSITE:

Item	Price	Notes

CHRISTMAS BAKING PLANNER

NOVEMBER						
Sunday	Monday	Tuesday	Wednesday	Thursday	Friday	Saturday

DECEMBER						
Sunday	Monday	Tuesday	Wednesday	Thursday	Friday	Saturday

BAKING SHOPPING LIST

Baking Supplies

- [ ] _____
- [ ] _____
- [ ] _____
- [ ] _____
- [ ] _____
- [ ] _____
- [ ] _____
- [ ] _____
- [ ] _____
- [ ] _____
- [ ] _____
- [ ] _____
- [ ] _____
- [ ] _____
- [ ] _____
- [ ] _____

Dairy

- [ ] _____
- [ ] _____
- [ ] _____
- [ ] _____
- [ ] _____
- [ ] _____
- [ ] _____

Canned Goods

- [ ] _____
- [ ] _____
- [ ] _____
- [ ] _____
- [ ] _____
- [ ] _____
- [ ] _____

Frozen Foods

- [ ] _____
- [ ] _____
- [ ] _____
- [ ] _____
- [ ] _____
- [ ] _____
- [ ] _____

Other

- [ ] _____
- [ ] _____
- [ ] _____
- [ ] _____
- [ ] _____
- [ ] _____
- [ ] _____
- [ ] _____

RECIPE

INGREDIENTS	

INSTRUCTIONS

COMMENTS RECEIVED

RATING ☆☆☆☆☆	MAKE AGAIN? Yes No

RECIPE

INGREDIENTS	

INSTRUCTIONS

COMMENTS RECEIVED

RATING ☆☆☆☆☆	MAKE AGAIN? Yes No

RECIPE

_____

INGREDIENTS	

INSTRUCTIONS

COMMENTS RECEIVED

RATING ☆☆☆☆☆	MAKE AGAIN? Yes No

RECIPE

INGREDIENTS	

INSTRUCTIONS

COMMENTS RECEIVED			
RATING ☆☆☆☆☆	MAKE AGAIN?	Yes	No

RECIPE

INGREDIENTS	

INSTRUCTIONS

COMMENTS RECEIVED	
RATING ☆☆☆☆☆	MAKE AGAIN? Yes No

RECIPE

INGREDIENTS	

INSTRUCTIONS

COMMENTS RECEIVED		
RATING ☆☆☆☆☆	MAKE AGAIN? Yes	No

RECIPE

INGREDIENTS	

INSTRUCTIONS

COMMENTS RECEIVED

RATING ☆☆☆☆☆	MAKE AGAIN? Yes No

RECIPE

INGREDIENTS	

INSTRUCTIONS

COMMENTS RECEIVED			
RATING ☆☆☆☆☆	MAKE AGAIN?	Yes	No

RECIPE

INGREDIENTS	

INSTRUCTIONS

COMMENTS RECEIVED	
RATING ☆☆☆☆☆	MAKE AGAIN? Yes No

RECIPE

INGREDIENTS	

INSTRUCTIONS

COMMENTS RECEIVED			
RATING ☆☆☆☆☆	MAKE AGAIN?	Yes	No

CHRISTMAS DECORATIONS INVENTORY

For the Tree	For Outside
☐ Tree	☐ Lights
☐ Tree Skirt	☐ Wreaths
☐ Lights	☐ Wreath Hangers
☐ Garland	☐ Yard Decorations
☐ Tree Topper	☐
☐ Ornaments	☐
☐	☐
☐	☐
☐	☐
For the Table	**For Around the House**
☐ Place Mats	☐ Stockings
☐ Table Runner	☐ Stocking Hangers
☐ Napkins	☐ Candles
☐ Table Cloth	☐ Christmas Music
☐ Dishes	☐ Christmas Books
☐ Serving Dishes	☐
☐ Napkin Rings	☐
☐	☐
☐	☐
Storage Notes	**Items to Buy**
	☐
	☐
	☐
	☐
	☐
	☐
	☐
	☐

DECORATIONS PLANNER

Living Room	Dining Room
Kitchen	Bathroom
Bedrooms	Guestroom
Hallway	Staircase
Foyer	Den
Other	Other

CHRISTMAS MENU PLANNER

Date

Guests

- ☐
- ☐
- ☐
- ☐
- ☐
- ☐
- ☐
- ☐
- ☐
- ☐
- ☐
- ☐
- ☐

Main Dishes

Salads

Side Dishes & Condiments

Breads

Desserts

Beverages	Dishes Others are Bringing	Place Settings

Grocery List

- ☐
- ☐
- ☐
- ☐
- ☐
- ☐

- ☐
- ☐
- ☐
- ☐
- ☐
- ☐

- ☐
- ☐
- ☐
- ☐
- ☐
- ☐

CHRISTMAS MENU PLANNER

Date

Guests

- ☐
- ☐
- ☐
- ☐
- ☐
- ☐
- ☐
- ☐
- ☐
- ☐
- ☐
- ☐
- ☐

Main Dishes

Salads

Side Dishes & Condiments

Breads

Desserts

Beverages	Dishes Others are Bringing	Place Settings

Grocery List

- ☐
- ☐
- ☐
- ☐
- ☐
- ☐

- ☐
- ☐
- ☐
- ☐
- ☐
- ☐

- ☐
- ☐
- ☐
- ☐
- ☐
- ☐

CHRISTMAS MENU PLANNER

Date

Guests

☐
☐
☐
☐
☐
☐
☐
☐
☐
☐
☐
☐
☐

Main Dishes

Salads

Side Dishes & Condiments

Breads

Desserts

Beverages	Dishes Others are Bringing	Place Settings

Grocery List

☐   ☐   ☐
☐   ☐   ☐
☐   ☐   ☐
☐   ☐   ☐
☐   ☐   ☐
☐   ☐   ☐

CHRISTMAS MENU PLANNER

Date	Main Dishes
Guests	
☐	
☐	**Salads**
☐	
☐	
☐	**Side Dishes & Condiments**
☐	
☐	
☐	**Breads**
☐	
☐	
☐	**Desserts**
☐	
☐	

Beverages	Dishes Others are Bringing	Place Settings

Grocery List

☐	☐	☐
☐	☐	☐
☐	☐	☐
☐	☐	☐
☐	☐	☐
☐	☐	☐

CHRISTMAS EVE PLANS

EVENING PLANS		
Activity	Time/Location	Remember to Take

TO DO BEFORE KIDS GO TO BED		
☐	☐	☐
☐	☐	☐
☐	☐	☐
☐	☐	☐
☐	☐	☐

TO DO AFTER KIDS GO TO BED		
☐	☐	☐
☐	☐	☐
☐	☐	☐
☐	☐	☐
☐	☐	☐

ITEMS TO PREPARE FOR CHRISTMAS DAY		
☐	☐	☐
☐	☐	☐
☐	☐	☐
☐	☐	☐
☐	☐	☐
☐	☐	☐

CHRISTMAS DAY PLANS

TO DO LIST		
☐	☐	☐
☐	☐	☐
☐	☐	☐
☐	☐	☐
☐	☐	☐

MORNING PLANS		
Activity	Time/Location	Remember to Take

AFTERNOON PLANS		
Activity	Time/Location	Remember to Take

EVENING PLANS		
Activity	Time/Location	Remember to Take

COMPANY'S COMING

Who is Coming	Arrival Date
	Departure Date

Pick Up Arrangements
Dietary Issues to Note
Sleeping Arrangements to Prepare

Shopping List

- ☐ _____
- ☐ _____
- ☐ _____
- ☐ _____
- ☐ _____
- ☐ _____
- ☐ _____
- ☐ _____
- ☐ _____
- ☐ _____
- ☐ _____
- ☐ _____
- ☐ _____
- ☐ _____
- ☐ _____
- ☐ _____
- ☐ _____
- ☐ _____
- ☐ _____

Menu Plans

_____
_____
_____
_____
_____
_____
_____
_____
_____
_____

To Do List

- ☐ _____
- ☐ _____
- ☐ _____
- ☐ _____
- ☐ _____
- ☐ _____
- ☐ _____
- ☐ _____
- ☐ _____
- ☐ _____

COMPANY'S COMING

Who is Coming	Arrival Date
	Departure Date

Pick Up Arrangements
Dietary Issues to Note
Sleeping Arrangements to Prepare

Shopping List

☐ _____
☐ _____
☐ _____
☐ _____
☐ _____
☐ _____
☐ _____
☐ _____
☐ _____
☐ _____
☐ _____
☐ _____
☐ _____
☐ _____
☐ _____
☐ _____
☐ _____

Menu Plans

_____
_____
_____
_____
_____
_____
_____

To Do List

☐ _____
☐ _____
☐ _____
☐ _____
☐ _____
☐ _____
☐ _____
☐ _____
☐ _____

PARTY PLANS

Theme	Date
Decorations	
Parking Arrangements	
Dietary Issues to Note	
Entertainment	

Guest List

☐ _____
☐ _____
☐ _____
☐ _____
☐ _____
☐ _____
☐ _____
☐ _____
☐ _____
☐ _____
☐ _____
☐ _____
☐ _____
☐ _____
☐ _____
☐ _____
☐ _____
☐ _____
☐ _____

Menu Plans

_____
_____
_____
_____
_____
_____
_____
_____

To Do List

☐ _____
☐ _____
☐ _____
☐ _____
☐ _____
☐ _____
☐ _____
☐ _____

POST PARTY NOTES

Best Moments

Insights About the Decorations

Insights About the Food & Drink

Insights About the Guest List

Recommendations for Next Time

PARTY PLANS

Theme	Date
Decorations	
Parking Arrangements	
Dietary Issues to Note	
Entertainment	

Guest List

- _____
- _____
- _____
- _____
- _____
- _____
- _____
- _____
- _____
- _____
- _____
- _____
- _____
- _____
- _____
- _____
- _____
- _____
- _____

Menu Plans

_____
_____
_____
_____
_____
_____
_____
_____

To Do List

- _____
- _____
- _____
- _____
- _____
- _____
- _____
- _____
- _____

POST PARTY NOTES

Best Moments

Insights About the Decorations

Insights About the Food & Drink

Insights About the Guest List

Recommendations for Next Time

PARTY PLANS

Theme	Date
Decorations	
Parking Arrangements	
Dietary Issues to Note	
Entertainment	

Guest List

- [ ]
- [ ]
- [ ]
- [ ]
- [ ]
- [ ]
- [ ]
- [ ]
- [ ]
- [ ]
- [ ]
- [ ]
- [ ]
- [ ]
- [ ]
- [ ]
- [ ]
- [ ]

Menu Plans

To Do List

- [ ]
- [ ]
- [ ]
- [ ]
- [ ]
- [ ]
- [ ]
- [ ]

POST PARTY NOTES

Best Moments

Insights About the Decorations

Insights About the Food & Drink

Insights About the Guest List

Recommendations for Next Time

OUTFIT PLANNER

Date	Occasion	Outfit is for
Main Outfit	Shoes	Accessories
Hairstyle	Makeup	Notes

Date	Occasion	Outfit for
Main Outfit	Shoes	Accessories
Hairstyle	Makeup	Notes

OUTFIT PLANNER

Date	Occasion	Outfit for
Main Outfit	Shoes	Accessories
Hairstyle	Makeup	Notes

Date	Occasion	Outfit for
Main Outfit	Shoes	Accessories
Hairstyle	Makeup	Notes

OUTFIT PLANNER

Date	Occasion	Outfit for
Main Outfit	Shoes	Accessories
Hairstyle	Makeup	Notes

Date	Occasion	Outfit for
Main Outfit	Shoes	Accessories
Hairstyle	Makeup	Notes

OUTFIT PLANNER

Date	Occasion	Outfit for
Main Outfit	Shoes	Accessories
Hairstyle	Makeup	Notes

Date	Occasion	Outfit for
Main Outfit	Shoes	Accessories
Hairstyle	Makeup	Notes

CHRISTMAS BUDGET

TOTAL BUDGET AMOUNT: $_____		
Gift Budget		
Family	$	Notes
Friends	$	
Coworkers	$	
Neighbors	$	
Other People	$	
Gift Wrapping	$	
Cards & Decorations Budget		
Cards	$	Notes
Photos	$	
Postage	$	
Tree	$	
House Decorations	$	
Party Decorations	$	
Other	$	
Food Budget		
Baking	$	Notes
Christmas Dinner	$	
Party Food/Drink	$	
Dining Out	$	
Christmas Eve	$	
Other	$	
Activities Budget		
	$	Notes
	$	
	$	
	$	
	$	

CHRISTMAS BUDGET (Continued)

New Year's Budget		
Activity	$	Notes
Food/Drink	$	
Decorations	$	
Other	$	
Clothing Budget		
	$	Notes
	$	
	$	
	$	
	$	
	$	
Miscellaneous Budget		
	$	Notes
	$	
	$	
	$	
	$	
	$	

Notes

CRISTMAS MOVIES TO WATCH

☐ _____ RATING ☆☆☆☆☆

☐ _____ RATING ☆☆☆☆☆

☐ _____ RATING ☆☆☆☆☆

☐ _____ RATING ☆☆☆☆☆

☐ _____ RATING ☆☆☆☆☆

☐ _____ RATING ☆☆☆☆☆

☐ _____ RATING ☆☆☆☆☆

☐ _____ RATING ☆☆☆☆☆

☐ _____ RATING ☆☆☆☆☆

☐ _____ RATING ☆☆☆☆☆

☐ _____ RATING ☆☆☆☆☆

☐ _____ RATING ☆☆☆☆☆

☐ _____ RATING ☆☆☆☆☆

☐ _____ RATING ☆☆☆☆☆

☐ _____ RATING ☆☆☆☆☆

☐ _____ RATING ☆☆☆☆☆

☐ _____ RATING ☆☆☆☆☆

☐ _____ RATING ☆☆☆☆☆

☐ _____ RATING ☆☆☆☆☆

☐ _____ RATING ☆☆☆☆☆

☐ _____ RATING ☆☆☆☆☆

☐ _____ RATING ☆☆☆☆☆

☐ _____ RATING ☆☆☆☆☆

☐ _____ RATING ☆☆☆☆☆

☐ _____ RATING ☆☆☆☆☆

CRISTMAS MOVIES TO WATCH

☐ _____ RATING ☆☆☆☆☆

☐ _____ RATING ☆☆☆☆☆

☐ _____ RATING ☆☆☆☆☆

☐ _____ RATING ☆☆☆☆☆

☐ _____ RATING ☆☆☆☆☆

☐ _____ RATING ☆☆☆☆☆

☐ _____ RATING ☆☆☆☆☆

☐ _____ RATING ☆☆☆☆☆

☐ _____ RATING ☆☆☆☆☆

☐ _____ RATING ☆☆☆☆☆

☐ _____ RATING ☆☆☆☆☆

☐ _____ RATING ☆☆☆☆☆

☐ _____ RATING ☆☆☆☆☆

☐ _____ RATING ☆☆☆☆☆

☐ _____ RATING ☆☆☆☆☆

☐ _____ RATING ☆☆☆☆☆

☐ _____ RATING ☆☆☆☆☆

☐ _____ RATING ☆☆☆☆☆

☐ _____ RATING ☆☆☆☆☆

☐ _____ RATING ☆☆☆☆☆

☐ _____ RATING ☆☆☆☆☆

☐ _____ RATING ☆☆☆☆☆

☐ _____ RATING ☆☆☆☆☆

☐ _____ RATING ☆☆☆☆☆

☐ _____ RATING ☆☆☆☆☆

CHRISTMAS MEMORIES

CHRISTMAS MEMORIES

CHRISTMAS MEMORIES

CHRISTMAS MEMORIES

CHRISTMAS MEMORIES

CHRISTMAS MEMORIES

CHRISTMAS MEMORIES

CHRISTMAS MEMORIES

CHRISTMAS MEMORIES

CHRISTMAS MEMORIES

CHRISTMAS MEMORIES

CHRISTMAS MEMORIES

CHRISTMAS MEMORIES

CHRISTMAS MEMORIES

CHRISTMAS MEMORIES

CHRISTMAS MEMORIES

CHRISTMAS MEMORIES

CHRISTMAS MEMORIES

CHRISTMAS MEMORIES

CHRISTMAS MEMORIES

CHRISTMAS MEMORIES

CHRISTMAS MEMORIES

CHRISTMAS SKETCHES & MEMENTOS

CHRISTMAS SKETCHES & MEMENTOS

CHRISTMAS SKETCHES & MEMENTOS

CHRISTMAS SKETCHES & MEMENTOS

CHRISTMAS SKETCHES & MEMENTOS

CHRISTMAS SKETCHES & MEMENTOS

CHRISTMAS SKETCHES & MEMENTOS

CHRISTMAS SKETCHES & MEMENTOS

CHRISTMAS SKETCHES & MEMENTOS

CHRISTMAS SKETCHES & MEMENTOS

CHRISTMAS SKETCHES & MEMENTOS

CHRISTMAS SKETCHES & MEMENTOS

CHRISTMAS SKETCHES & MEMENTOS

CHRISTMAS SKETCHES & MEMENTOS

CHRISTMAS SKETCHES & MEMENTOS

CHRISTMAS SKETCHES & MEMENTOS

CHRISTMAS SKETCHES & MEMENTOS

CHRISTMAS SKETCHES & MEMENTOS

CHRISTMAS SKETCHES & MEMENTOS

CHRISTMAS SKETCHES & MEMENTOS

CHRISTMAS SKETCHES & MEMENTOS

CHRISTMAS SKETCHES & MEMENTOS

QUICK REFERENCE

Made in the USA
Monee, IL
07 September 2020

41127264R00070